OWL'S NUMBER SCHOOL

illustrated by Pam Adams

Child's Play (International) Ltd
© 1983 M. Twinn   ISBN 0-85953-166-X   Printed in S

1
one
cat

2
two
dogs

3
three
goats

ts, dogs, goats, bears, rabbits and ducks.

5
five
rabbits

4
four
bears

6
six
ducklings

7
seven frogs

8
eight fish

9
nine snakes

gs, fish, snakes, caterpillars, moths and bees.

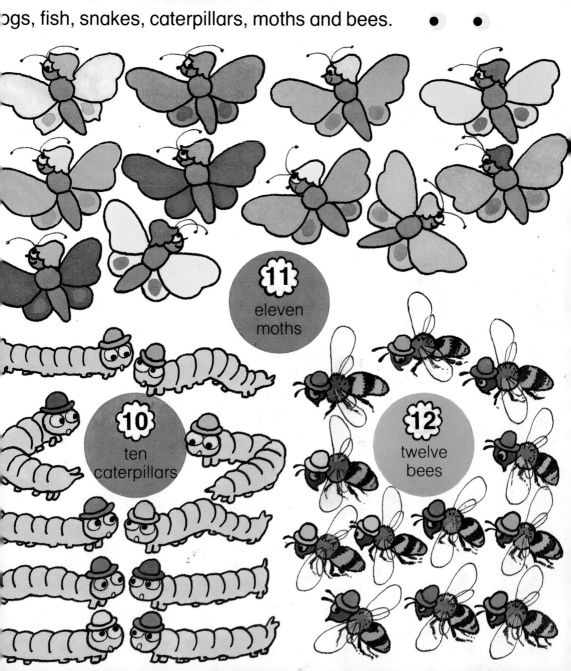

11 eleven moths

10 ten caterpillars

12 twelve bees

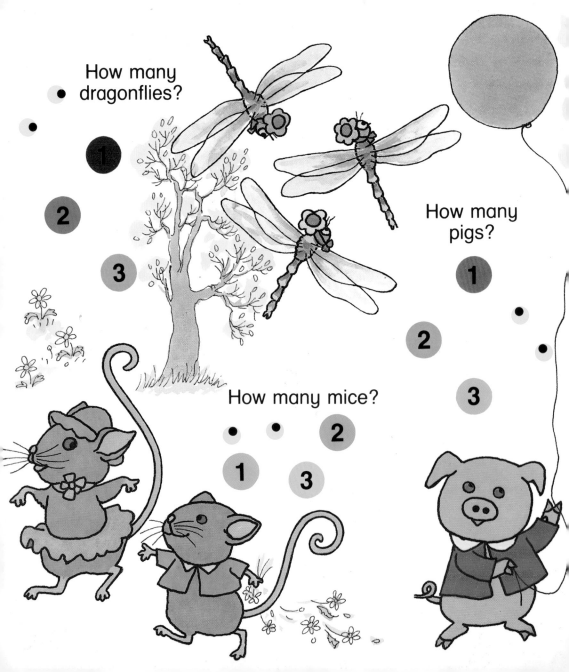

How many dragonflies?

How many pigs?

How many mice?

How many birds?

1 2 3

How many hedgehogs?

3 1 2

How many rabbits?

2 3 1

How many
trapeze
artists?

2

1   **4**   **3**

How many
clowns?

1   **3**

2   **4**

How many
horses?

4   **1**

2

3

How many
lions?

1 2 3 4

How many
elephants?

1 2 3 4

How many
dogs?

1 2 3 4

How many trays?

4   5   2   1   3

How many nurses?

3   2   1   4   5

How many visitors?

5   4   3   1   2

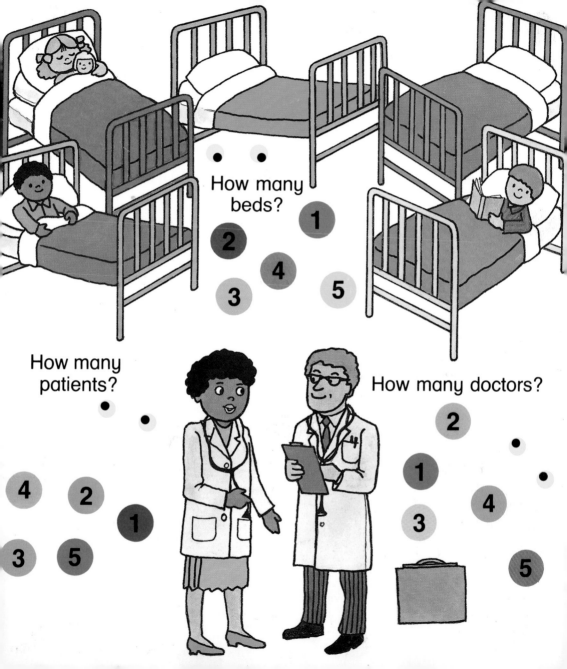

How many beds?

How many patients?

How many doctors?

How many presents?

How many candles?

How many hats?

How many
balloons?

2
3
1
4
6
5

How many
ice-creams?

2
1
6
3
4
5

How many
children?

6
5
4
1
2
3

How many
tables?

7 8 9

How many
chairs?

8

7

9

How many children?

7 8 9

How many
pictures?

7

8

9

How many books?

7 8 9

How many crayons?

7 8 9

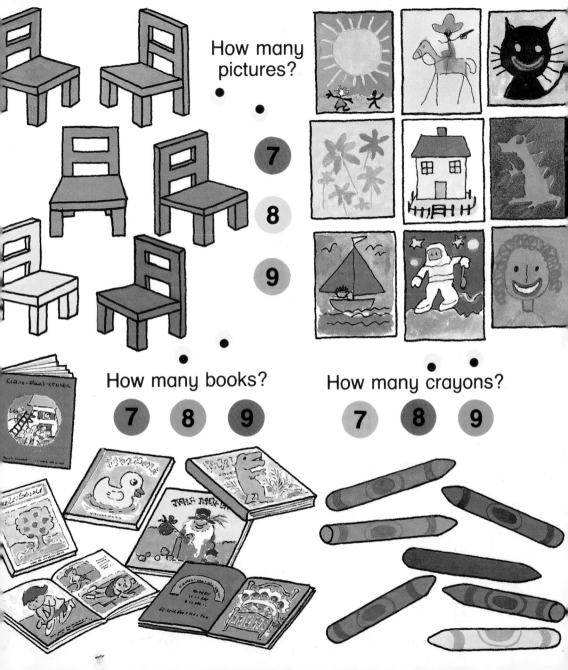

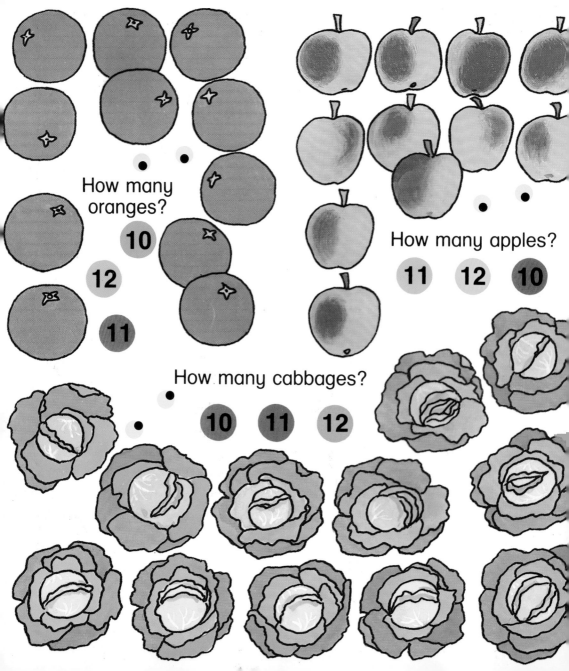

How many
oranges?

10
12
11

How many apples?

11 12 10

How many cabbages?

10 11 12

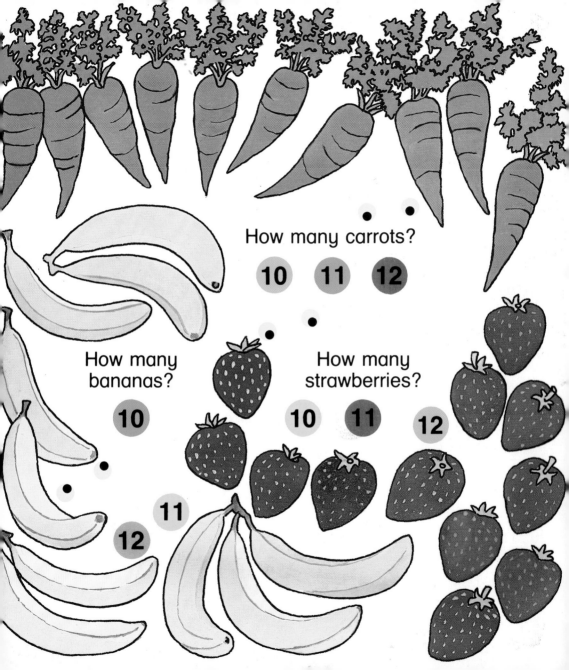

How many carrots?

10 **11** **12**

How many bananas?

10

11

12

How many strawberries?

10 **11** **12**

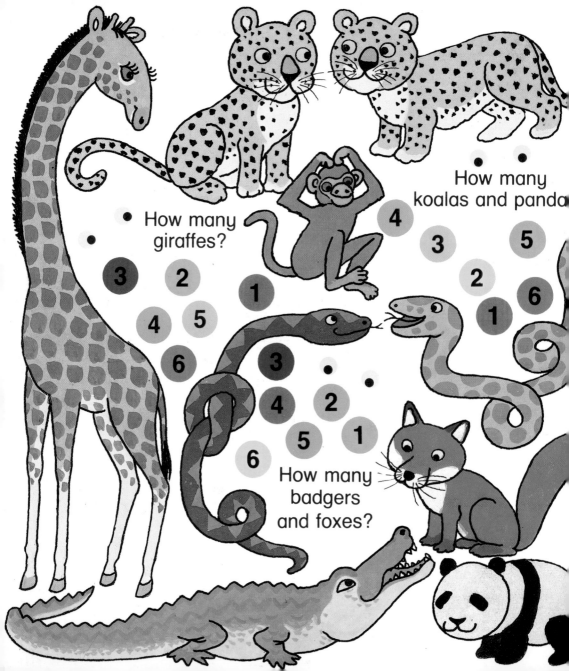

How many
giraffes?

3 2 1
4 5
6

How many
koalas and panda[s]

4 3 5
2 6
1

3 2 1
4
5
6

How many
badgers
and foxes?

How many leopards and zebras?

How many monkeys?

How many snakes and crocodiles?

How many
lions and tigers?

8 7
9 12
10 11

How many
kangaroos and camels?

8 7
9 12
10 11

How many
parrots and penguins?

7
8 9 10
12 11